What Is the Women's Rights Movement?

by Deborah Hopkinson

illustrated by Laurie A. Conley

Penguin Workshop
An Imprint of Penguin Random House

For Alice Paul and her family, and in loving
memory of her great aunt Michele—DH

In honor of the brave and interesting
women I learned about while researching
the drawings for this book—LAC

PENGUIN WORKSHOP
Penguin Young Readers Group
An Imprint of Penguin Random House LLC

Library of Congress Cataloging-in-Publication Data is available.

ISBN 9781524786298 (paperback)   10 9 8 7 6 5 4 3 2 1
ISBN 9781524786311 (library binding)   10 9 8 7 6 5 4 3 2 1

Contents

What Is the Women's Rights Movement?

You might not expect an old cemetery to be a busy place on Election Day in the United States. But 2016 was different.

For the first time, a woman was running for US president from one of the two major political parties. It was Democrat Hillary Clinton. Her nomination was a milestone in the struggle of American women to achieve equality with men.

To celebrate, visitors streamed to Mount Hope Cemetery in Rochester, New York. They wanted to honor the memory of Susan B. Anthony. She was an early women's rights leader. People lined up to place flowers and flags on the grass. Soon, "I Voted" stickers covered the simple gravestone.

Susan would have been delighted. She devoted her life to the cause of women's *suffrage*—the right to vote. Once, in 1872, Susan voted in a presidential election. It was illegal back then, and she was arrested. One newspaper published an illustration of her with the title "The Woman Who Dared."

A judge sentenced her to pay a hundred dollars. Susan told him she'd "never pay a dollar of your unjust penalty." She never did.

Susan B. Anthony didn't live to see her dream come true. American women didn't win the right to vote until 1920. That was fourteen years after she passed away.

And although Hillary Clinton's campaign in 2016 made history, she didn't win the election. No woman has ever been elected president or vice president of the United States . . . at least not yet.

As Susan once said, "Failure is impossible."

CHAPTER 1
Early America

On March 31, 1776, Abigail Adams picked up a quill pen to write to her husband, John. It was a dangerous time. The thirteen colonies in America wanted to separate from England to form their own country.

John Adams was often away at the Continental Congress in Philadelphia. John was there to help write the Declaration of Independence and discuss how the government of the new United States of America would work. Abigail stayed home in Massachusetts to care for their children and farm.

Still, Abigail had a keen interest in plans for the new nation. And she often shared her ideas with John. For one thing, Abigail believed slavery was wrong. By 1810, the number of enslaved people in the United States—almost all living in the South—totaled more than a million.

Abigail also spoke out for women. At the time, women in America had few rights. When a woman married, she suffered something called "a civil death." This wasn't a real death, of course. But the law didn't recognize her as a separate person anymore. It meant that a married woman couldn't own property. She had to turn any money she earned over to her husband. Divorce was rare. However, if a couple did separate, in most cases fathers gained custody of their children.

Abigail didn't like any of these rules. She hoped John and the other Founders would make different laws for the new nation. And so she wrote, urging John to "remember the ladies, and be more generous and favorable to them than your ancestors." Abigail added, "Do not put such unlimited power into the hands of husbands."

John wrote back, half joking, "Depend on

it, we know better than to repeal our masculine systems." In other words, even loving husbands like John Adams wanted to keep society the way it was.

The Founders were bold men. But perhaps Abigail Adams was bolder. For she also told John she thought women would start a rebellion someday against laws "in which we have no voice or representation."

The Founders

Abigail Adams was right. In 1848, only thirty years after her death, the women's rights movement began. And it was another busy wife and mother who set things in motion.

CHAPTER 2
The Seneca Falls Convention

Elizabeth Cady married Henry Stanton on May 1, 1840. Even as a twenty-four-year-old bride, Elizabeth was already questioning her role as a woman. She left out the word *obey* from her wedding vows. She also kept using her name, becoming known as Elizabeth Cady Stanton.

Her husband, Henry, was a well-known abolitionist. That means a person working to *abolish*—to end—slavery in America. However, even at an abolitionist convention they attended, the men refused to allow women to take part. Elizabeth felt outraged. So did another woman named Lucretia Mott. Shouldn't women be treated as equal partners in the fight against slavery?

Elizabeth and Lucretia decided to do something for women's rights. It was eight years before they were able to begin. By then, Elizabeth was a busy mother. The family lived in Seneca Falls, a town in upstate New York.

On Sunday, July 9, 1848, Elizabeth, Lucretia, and three friends gathered together. Elizabeth poured out her frustrations about the unfair treatment of women. She proposed "a public meeting for protest and discussion."

Her friend Lucretia and the others felt the same. Right away, they got started. They wrote a notice for the newspaper announcing a "Women's Rights Convention" for July 19 and 20—the very next week! There wasn't much time to plan. What should they say?

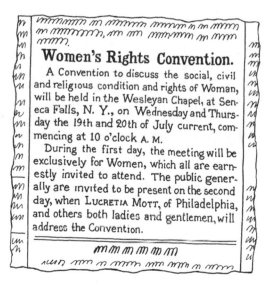

Women's Rights Convention.

A Convention to discuss the social, civil and religious condition and rights of Woman, will be held in the Wesleyan Chapel, at Seneca Falls, N. Y., on Wednesday and Thursday the 19th and 20th of July current, commencing at 10 o'clock A. M.

During the first day, the meeting will be exclusively for Women, which all are earnestly invited to attend. The public generally are invited to be present on the second day, when LUCRETIA MOTT, of Philadelphia, and others both ladies and gentlemen, will address the Convention.

Elizabeth decided to use the Declaration of Independence as a model. She called her version the Declaration of Sentiments. She wrote: "We hold these truths to be self-evident: that all men **and women** are created equal."

Elizabeth's Declaration of Sentiments included eleven demands for action. One was for suffrage. This was a shocking idea at the time. Women couldn't vote anywhere in the world! The demand was so bold, her husband refused to attend the women's first meeting.

Elizabeth held firm. Her father was a judge, and she'd grown up reading his law books. Elizabeth understood that the best way to change society was to change its laws. Without the legal right to vote, women could never be full citizens.

Even on such short notice, more than three hundred people, including about forty men, flocked to the Wesleyan Chapel in Seneca Falls.

It was July 20, 1848. Elizabeth read aloud the Declaration of Sentiments.

When she got to the part about women voting, she declared, "The right is ours. Have it, we must. Use it, we will."

At first, this idea didn't go over well. Then one man spoke up in support: the great African American leader Frederick Douglass. In his abolitionist newspaper, *The North Star*, Douglass wrote that "there can be no reason in the world"

to deny women the vote.

In the end, one hundred people at the Seneca Falls Convention—sixty-eight women and thirty-two men—supported the right to women's suffrage.

Years later, Frederick Douglass reflected that it had taken women a lot of "moral courage" to demand the vote. It was not easy to start such a campaign, he said, "with one-half the whole world against you, as these women did."

Frederick Douglass was right: Many people were against women's rights. After the Seneca Falls Convention, one newspaper said the changes women wanted were "impractical, uncalled for, and unnecessary." Another declared, "A woman is nobody. A wife is everything." In other words, women belonged at home.

But Elizabeth soon found another friend who shared her dedication to women's rights. Her name was Susan B. Anthony.

Frederick Douglass (1818–1895)

Frederick Douglass was born into slavery in Maryland in 1818. He learned to read and secretly

taught other slaves. He escaped in 1838 by using false papers and pretending to be a sailor.

In 1845, he published the story of his life, *Narrative of the Life of Frederick Douglass*. By showing the evils of slavery, the book helped convince more Americans that slavery must be abolished.

Frederick Douglass had a vision for an America where everyone was equal. He dedicated his life to that cause. He died in 1895.

CHAPTER 3
Elizabeth and Susan

Susan B. Anthony was born in Massachusetts on February 15, 1820. Her family was Quaker, part of a religious movement that believes in peace, justice, and equality.

Quakers also supported education for girls. Susan's father owned a mill and started a school for the girls and women who worked there. Susan herself started teaching part-time in her teens. Later she supported herself as a teacher.

Although she had suitors, Susan never married. She once said, "I never felt I could give up my life of freedom to become a man's housekeeper."

One day in 1851, Susan visited Seneca Falls with her friend Amelia Bloomer. Amelia introduced Susan to Elizabeth. It was the beginning of a lifelong friendship that changed history.

Bloomers

In the nineteenth century, a woman's clothes were designed to give her an hourglass shape with a tiny waist. Women wore stiff, tight-fitting undergarments called *corsets*. Corsets made it hard to breathe!

Some women began to wear loose pants under a short dress. The pants were called *bloomers*, after Amelia, who started the look. Although bloomers didn't really catch on, over time women's fashion did "loosen up."

As the women's rights movement grew in the 1850s, Susan and Elizabeth became its leaders. They made a great team.

Elizabeth had seven children and couldn't travel easily. Susan could—and did. Susan once said, "When she forged the firebolts, I fired them." In other words, Elizabeth wrote the speeches, and Susan gave them.

And Susan certainly gave lots of speeches! In the first five months of 1855 alone, she visited fifty-four counties in New York State. Susan braved cold, snow, and bad roads.

One newspaper editor accused Susan of trying to "poison the morals" of girls. Even some women were against suffrage. One said Susan had turned her back on her true role in life: being a wife and mother.

In addition to speaking out for women's rights, Susan gave speeches about the need to end slavery. Other women, including African American leader and former slave Sojourner Truth, were also active in both causes. In 1851, Sojourner spoke at the Ohio Women's Rights Convention. Her powerful words were unforgettable. She declared, "I

Sojourner Truth

could work as much and eat as much as a man— when I could get it—and bear the lash as well.

And ain't I a woman?" She was saying that women were the equals of men.

In 1860, Abraham Lincoln was elected president. By this time, one issue was on everyone's minds. And it wasn't women's right to vote.

Slavery was about to break America apart.

CHAPTER 4
A Long, Hard Fight

In April 1861, the Civil War began. Eleven Southern states withdrew from the United States to form their own country—the Confederate States of America, where slavery would continue. The war lasted for four years and left more than 620,000 dead.

Women couldn't serve in the military, but several hundred disguised themselves as men in order to fight. Others found different ways to join the war effort. Clara Barton, who later founded the American Red Cross, was the most famous Civil

Clara Barton

War nurse. She braved bullets to help wounded soldiers. Former slave Susie King Taylor was the first black US Army nurse, serving African American soldiers in a Union regiment.

Susie King Taylor

Peace came in 1865 when the South surrendered. All former slaves were now free. During the war, Susan and Elizabeth had been forced to put women's rights work on hold. Now they hoped the reunified country was ready for universal suffrage. They wanted Congress to *amend*, or change, the US Constitution and make it the law that *all* adults—black and white, men and women—had the right to vote.

But almost everyone else thought the country wasn't ready yet. This was black men's hour—their time to gain suffrage. Elizabeth disagreed, declaring, "This is the nation's hour."

The Fifteenth Amendment said the right to vote couldn't be denied to citizens because of race. But only men were considered citizens. So because the Fifteenth Amendment still left out all women, Elizabeth and Susan felt they couldn't support it.

Others who were for women's suffrage had a different view. They argued that extending voting rights was progress—even if those rights didn't yet include women. Besides, what was the sense of not giving black men the right to vote?

There were so many fierce arguments that in 1869, the women's movement split into two rival groups. Elizabeth and Susan formed the National Woman Suffrage Association. Their goal was still to change the Constitution.

Lucy Stone and her husband, Henry Blackwell, created the American Woman Suffrage Association. This group supported the Fifteenth Amendment, which passed in 1870. Lucy and her friends also wanted to keep fighting for women. But they decided to work for the vote in a different way from Elizabeth and Susan's group.

Lucy Stone

Lucy knew the states had the power to say who could vote. She and her followers decided to spend their time trying to change laws in each state, one by one, until there was suffrage everywhere in the United States.

Meanwhile, Susan was urging women to vote in the 1872 presidential election. On November 1, 1872, she, her three sisters, and several other women persuaded some men who were signing up voters to let them register. Susan promised that if they were fined, she'd pay it. She must have been very convincing!

Then, on Election Day in Rochester, Susan and a few other women went to a polling place in a local general store. They demanded ballots—and voted. Susan told Elizabeth, "Well, I have been and gone and done it!"

Of course, what Susan had done was illegal. As she expected, Susan was arrested. Bail was set at five hundred dollars. Susan actually wanted to be

put in jail so she could bring her case to a higher
court. She didn't go to jail, which ruined her plan.
But there was a trial a few months later.

Judge Ward Hunt told the (all-male) jury to find her guilty. Before he passed the sentence, he asked if Susan had anything to say. Susan began, "Yes, Your Honor, I have many things to say."

She went on to tell the judge that he had "trampled underfoot every vital principle of our government. My natural rights, my civil rights, my political rights, my judicial rights, are all alike ignored."

Susan was fined one hundred dollars, which she never paid. Soon after, she and Elizabeth wrote their own amendment to the Constitution. It gave women the vote. A supporter introduced it in the US Congress in 1878.

Elizabeth was there in Washington, DC, and later recalled that none of the congressmen even paid attention! One senator "stretched, yawned, gazed at the ceiling, cut his nails, sharpened his pencil."

It was the first of many unsuccessful tries for a suffrage amendment. It became known as the "Anthony Amendment" in honor of Susan. It read: "The rights of citizens of the United States to vote shall not be denied or abridged by the United States or any state on account of sex."

Elizabeth and Susan kept on fighting, but they were getting old. In February 1906, at a celebration for Susan's eighty-sixth birthday, she told her friends not to give up. She declared, "Failure is impossible!"

Susan died a few weeks later.

CHAPTER 5
Getting an Education

When she was a girl, Elizabeth Cady Stanton could do everything the boys in her high school class did. She could jump fences on horseback, win prizes for Greek, and excel at mathematics.

But there was something Elizabeth couldn't do when she graduated in 1830. She couldn't go to the same college as the boys in her class. Girls weren't allowed. She did go for two years to a special all-girls' school called a *seminary*. Some of these schools, such as Mount Holyoke in Massachusetts, founded in 1837, later became regular colleges for women.

Mount Holyoke Seminary School

Mount Holyoke was the first of a group of seven women's colleges called "the Seven Sisters." These colleges offered an education that was just as good as what men were getting at places like Harvard and Yale. However, the costs were high, and many other colleges still didn't accept women. That meant very few girls could dream of earning a college degree. And without a degree, it was difficult to enter professions such as law or medicine. Still, determined women started breaking down barriers.

Elizabeth Blackwell was born in England in 1821 and moved to the United States as a girl. She dreamed of being a doctor, saying, "My mind is fully made up."

She applied to more than a dozen colleges before she was accepted in 1847 at Geneva Medical College in Geneva, New York. In 1849, Elizabeth became the first woman in the United States to get a medical degree, graduating at the

Elizabeth Blackwell

top of her class. Later, she started a small hospital and helped train women in medicine.

Mary Church Terrell (1863–1954)

Born in Tennessee in 1863 to former slaves, Mary Church Terrell graduated in 1884 from Oberlin College, one of the first colleges to admit  African Americans and women. She became an educator and founding president of the National Association of Colored Women in 1896 to support the rights of black women and their families. In 1898, Mary spoke at a suffrage meeting. She reminded her audience that when the women's rights movement began, most black girls and women lived in states that "made it a crime to teach them to read."

A tireless crusader, Mary Church Terrell took part in civil rights protests into her eighties. She died in 1954 at age ninety.

Maria Mitchell was an astronomer who discovered a comet in 1847. In 1848, she became the first woman elected to the American Academy of Arts and Sciences. She also was a professor at Vassar College (a Seven Sisters school) for twenty-three years. Maria held women's rights meetings in the college observatory, where she also inspired girls to study science.

Education Today

Women today make up about half of all college students in the United States. Women also earn about half of all *doctorates*—the most advanced degrees.

However, male professors are still paid more than women who hold the same rank. And as of 2014, women held only 31 percent of full-professor positions and made up less than 15 percent of presidents at major universities.

CHAPTER 6
Women at Work

Before the 1830s, nearly all women worked from home. They cooked and cleaned and cared for children. But in the nineteenth century, factories and mills began springing up in New England towns to turn cotton into cloth. Mill owners hired young women from nearby farms.

A bell woke the "mill girls" at four in the morning for a fourteen-hour day on the job. It was hard work, but there were some benefits. Young women could earn their own money and be more independent.

In 1844, female mill workers in Lowell, Massachusetts, formed one of the first US labor groups for women. They fought for better working conditions and a ten-hour workday.

By the end of the century, women made up about 20 percent of the total workforce in the country. More African American women worked than white women. In 1900, about 43 percent of black women worked, compared to about 18 percent of white women. Many black women could not afford to stop working after they got married. In 1900, only 3 percent of married white women worked.

There were many reasons for this. African American women had fewer chances to go to school. They were forced to take low-paid, unskilled jobs such as cooks, servants, and seamstresses.

The nineteenth century was also a time of immigration. Twelve million immigrants arrived in New York City between 1880 and 1930. About 70 percent of foreign-born single women worked to help support their families.

One was Pauline Newman, who was born in Lithuania in 1888. Schools there weren't open to her. Why? She was Jewish. When her family moved to New York City, she began working at about age nine. Girls and women worked long hours for low pay in unsafe factories. Pauline wanted to

help women improve their working conditions. In 1909, she helped organize thousands of women into the largest *strike*, or work stoppage, of American women to date. She continued fighting for fair treatment for employees as the first female organizer for the ILGWU (International Ladies' Garment Workers' Union).

Pauline had a long career bringing together women of all races and backgrounds. She believed they deserved a voice—and a vote—in making their workplaces and communities better.

Jane Addams (1860–1935)

Jane Addams was born in Illinois in 1860. She spent her life helping the poor and needy in Chicago. Most were immigrants.

Jane Addams was also active in the women's rights movement. She served as vice president of the National American Woman Suffrage Association from 1911 to 1914.

She said that immigrants and poor women living in cities should have the right to vote. Then they could help find solutions to local problems such as poor housing, dirty water, and bad working conditions in factories.

She encouraged world leaders to make peace agreements rather than start wars. In 1931, she won a Nobel Peace Prize, becoming the first American woman to win a Nobel Prize. She died in 1935.

CHAPTER 7
New Century, New Fight

By 1900, women had been fighting for suffrage for more than fifty years. In one speech, Jane Addams said women wanted to be doing important work in the world. Instead, they had to "start parades and hold meetings and maybe throw things before we get [the vote]."

Luckily, two new leaders, Carrie Chapman Catt and Alice Paul, were willing to keep holding meetings and parades. Carrie and Alice had different plans for how to win the vote. In the end, victory depended on them both.

Alice Paul

Carrie was born in 1859 and grew up in Iowa. After college, she became a teacher and a school superintendent.

Carrie got involved in women's suffrage at a key moment. In 1890, the two women's rights groups came together again to form one organization called the National American Woman Suffrage Association (NAWSA). Carrie was president from 1900 to 1904. She also served from 1915 to 1920.

Carrie Chapman Catt

In 1916, Carrie proposed what she called the "Winning Plan." Her idea was to bring together everyone working for suffrage: people trying to change the Constitution *and* those wanting to change laws in their home states.

In fact, women *were* slowly winning the right to vote in some states. Some women could vote only in local or state elections. But women were also gaining full suffrage—the right to vote in national elections for Congress and the president.

In 1869, the territory of Wyoming gave women full suffrage. In 1890, when it entered the union, Wyoming became the first state where women could vote for every office in the country. By 1914, women had full suffrage in eleven states: Wyoming, Colorado, Utah, Idaho, Oregon, Arizona, Nevada, Kansas, Montana, California, and Washington State.

But this progress was too slow for fiery young activist Alice Paul. Like Susan B. Anthony, Alice

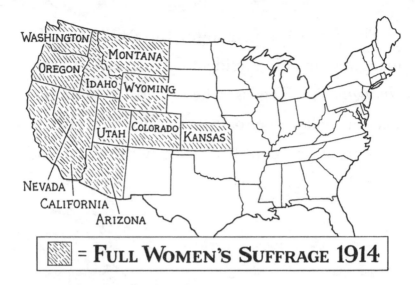

WASHINGTON
OREGON
MONTANA
IDAHO WYOMING
UTAH COLORADO KANSAS
NEVADA
CALIFORNIA
ARIZONA

▨ = **FULL WOMEN'S SUFFRAGE 1914**

grew up in a Quaker family. In 1912, she received a PhD from the University of Pennsylvania.

Alice also spent three years in England, where she took part in suffrage protest activities. (British women didn't obtain equal voting rights until 1928.) Alice brought daring new ideas back to America.

The best way to capture attention, Alice thought, was through newspaper stories. So she moved to Washington, DC, and set out to make news.

She planned a parade for the day before the inauguration of President Woodrow Wilson. (*Inauguration Day* is when whoever won the election takes the oath of office and begins working as president.) Alice knew the city would be packed with visitors.

The parade on March 3, 1913, *was* spectacular! It boasted eight thousand marchers as well as floats, cars, and horses. A wagon carried a gigantic banner proclaiming: "We Demand an Amendment to the Constitution of the United States Enfranchising the Women of this Country."

Like so many members of women's rights groups, most marchers were white. Some marchers, especially from the South, had wanted the parade to be segregated, with white and black women marching separately.

But black students from Howard University and leaders like Mary Church Terrell and Ida B. Wells objected. The college students wanted to walk with all other college students—and they did. Ida B. Wells marched alongside the white women from Illinois.

Ida B. Wells (1862–1931)

Ida B. Wells was born a slave on July 16, 1862, in Mississippi. When she was sixteen, Ida's parents and one of her brothers died. Ida worked to support her remaining five siblings.

Ida became a fearless journalist who investigated *lynchings*—the murder, usually by hanging, of black people by white mobs. She once said, "The  way to right wrongs is to turn the light of truth upon them." Writing for newspapers brought crimes to the attention of readers.

Ida married an attorney and raised a family in Chicago, where she remained active in civil and women's rights causes. Ida died in 1931.

Alice Paul's big parade made headlines. The *Washington Post* called it an "Entrancing Suffrage Appeal." Other newspapers praised the marchers' dignity when some men in the crowd blocked their way and shouted insults.

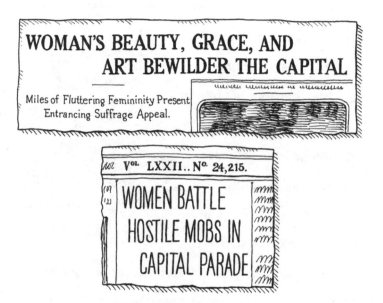

WOMAN'S BEAUTY, GRACE, AND ART BEWILDER THE CAPITAL

Miles of Fluttering Femininity Present Entrancing Suffrage Appeal.

Vᴼᴸ· LXXII.. Nᴼ· 24,215.

WOMEN BATTLE HOSTILE MOBS IN CAPITAL PARADE

Not everyone supported the march. One member of Congress declared the women "ought to have been at home." This antisuffrage view was shared even by women. There were many local antisuffrage organizations. In 1911, some of these groups merged to form the National Association Opposed to Woman Suffrage. (It disbanded after the vote was won.)

Woodrow Wilson

Alice didn't let this bother her. In fact, she welcomed drama and conflict. As the march proved, Alice wasn't afraid to confront Woodrow Wilson himself. She thought that if he put his support behind a suffrage amendment, Congress would follow.

She wanted the new president to be thinking about suffrage—every single day!

So in early 1917, Alice organized volunteers to *picket*, or march, in front of the White House. African American leader Mary Church Terrell was one of the picketers. But most volunteers were white single women.

Day after day, the women carried banners and protested in silence. One sign read: "Mr. President,

How Long Must Women Wait for Liberty?" As the months went on, the picketing continued. At first, President Wilson ignored the women. Then he just wished Alice and her picketers would go away.

But Alice would not go away—not until women had the vote.

CHAPTER 8
Victory at Last!

Alice Paul refused to stop her picketing campaign even after the United States entered World War I in April of 1917. That summer and fall, some picketers were arrested for no reason. Alice was among them.

Amazingly, she was sentenced to seven months in prison. In protest, Alice went on a hunger strike and was joined by several other women in jail for picketing. Their story captured the nation's attention.

Letters poured into the White House. President Wilson wanted to be seen as a leader for human rights around the globe. This was hard when American women were put in prison for demanding the right to vote.

That November, while Alice was in jail, suffrage passed in a New York State election. Winning the vote in a big state like New York helped to show that more people in the United States accepted suffrage.

Women's Suffrage around the World

In 1893, New Zealand became the first country to grant women suffrage. Then in 1902, Australia let white women vote. (But suffrage was denied to Aboriginal people—both male and female—until 1962.) Australia was followed by Finland in 1906, and Norway in 1913. Women could vote in Canada, Germany, Austria, and Poland by the end of 1918. Finally, in 2015, women in Saudi Arabia were able to vote.

Carrie Chapman Catt and her NAWSA group visited President Wilson. The women urged him to speak for an amendment to the Constitution.

Later that month, Alice—weak from hunger—and other prisoners were released from jail with no explanation.

All these events convinced President Wilson to take action. In January 1918, in Congress, he announced his support for a suffrage amendment to the Constitution. With that, Congress began

to move forward. Even then, it took another year to win the votes needed in both the House of Representatives and the Senate.

The House of Representatives voted in favor of the Nineteenth Amendment in May 1919. The measure passed the House by 304 to 89 votes. The Senate followed in June, passing the law by 56 to 25 votes.

The amendment's wording hadn't changed since Susan B. Anthony and Elizabeth Cady Stanton wrote it more than forty years earlier. Alice Paul said, "Freedom has come not as a gift, but as a triumph."

Even so, the vote for women was still not a sure thing. Before it could become law, the amendment had to be approved, or *ratified*, by thirty-six states. And some states were still against women voting. By the summer of 1920, thirty-five states had ratified the amendment. Seven had rejected it. In the Tennessee House of

Representatives, legislators were tied. One man would break that tie.

That man was the youngest House member, Harry T. Burn. Harry came from an antisuffrage district. He even wore a red rose, a sign that he was against suffrage. But hidden in his pocket, Harry had something else: a letter from his mother, Phoebe Ensminger Burn. She urged him to support suffrage.

When it was his turn, he called out, "Aye!"

Tennessee had voted yes. The Nineteenth Amendment became law on August 26, 1920.

At long last, women had the vote!

For the rest of her life, Alice Paul continued to devote her life to women's rights, including supporting an equal rights amendment to the Constitution. She died in 1977 at age ninety-two.

After the victory for women's suffrage, Carrie said, "Let us do our part to keep it a true and triumphant democracy." In 1920, she transformed NAWSA into a new organization called the League of Women Voters. Carrie died in 1947 at the age of eighty-eight.

Today, the League of Women Voters helps all Americans become more informed voters by learning about candidates and issues. Its motto is "Make Democracy Work."

Make democracy work. In a way, that's all women were saying from the very beginning.

CHAPTER 9
Women in World War II

In December 1941, the United States entered War World II, and the lives of millions of American women were about to change. First Lady Eleanor Roosevelt had said that, during World War II, American women would do all that was asked of them, and much, much more. She was right.

World War II (1939–1945)

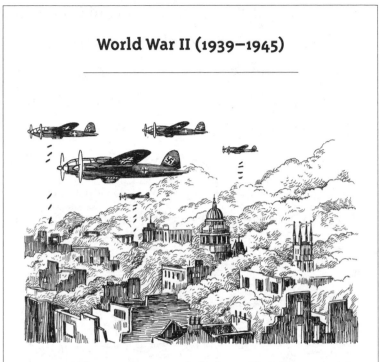

World War II was a global conflict from 1939 to 1945 that involved almost every part of the world. It pitted the Axis powers of Germany (led by Adolf Hitler), Italy, and Japan against the Allies, which included Great Britain, France, the United States, and the Soviet Union. It was the bloodiest war in history. More than fifty million people died before the Allies won in August 1945.

Before World War II, women could only join the military as nurses. While no women were in combat in World War II, they were definitely part of the US armed forces. In May 1942, Congress established what became the Women's Army Corps (WAC). During the war, about 150,000 women were WACs. They served as clerks, typists, and radio operators. They repaired trucks and drove vehicles.

About one hundred thousand women also joined the Navy as WAVES (Women Accepted for Volunteer Emergency Service). In addition to secretarial jobs, WAVES worked as translators and in coding and decoding messages. They were also air traffic controllers and weather forecasters.

More than eleven hundred women pilots volunteered to ferry planes from factories to military bases. They were known as WASPS, which stood for Women Airforce Service Pilots. The women flew every type of army aircraft. They also tested repaired planes to determine whether they were safe to fly.

To win the war, America needed more ships, planes, tanks, trucks, ammunition, and equipment. According to the National WWII museum, more than twelve million Americans served in the military. With so many men in uniform, who would work in the shipyards, plants, and factories?

Secretary of War Henry L. Stimson had a solution. Empty jobs would be filled by "the vast reserve of woman power." Six and a half million women worked outside the home in World War II.

A poster and song celebrated a fictional character called Rosie the Riveter. Rosie was the symbol of American women's patriotic spirit:

All the day long,
Whether rain or shine,
She's a part of the assembly line.
She's making history,
Working for victory,
Rosie the Riveter.

Women made uniforms and boots for soldiers.

They worked in factories to make silk parachutes.
Women produced ammunition on assembly lines.
They welded ships and airplanes.

During the war years, the United States produced three hundred thousand aircraft, eighty-six thousand tanks, and twelve thousand ships, along with millions of guns—all of which

couldn't have happened without women. Women proved they could do jobs that until then had only been done by men. About half of American women held jobs outside the home during the war.

In some factories, day care centers helped young mothers work both day and night shifts. These centers were new to Americans. Between 1942 and 1945, the government funded more than three thousand childcare centers serving six hundred thousand children.

Good factory jobs enabled black women to leave domestic service. As many as six hundred thousand African American women joined the war effort. In 1941, President Franklin D.

Roosevelt signed an executive order banning race discrimination in any business related to defense and war production. But this was often ignored.

Though racism still existed in the workplace, Ruth S. Wilson, a black sheet-metal worker and mother, said, "World War II changed my life because I made more money and became independent."

Like Ruth, millions of American women felt a new sense of independence during this time. They succeeded in new roles and occupations.

But when the war ended, millions of men returned to civilian life. Most people expected life to return to "normal." And often, especially for white middle-class families, that meant men went to work while women stayed home as wives and mothers. Throughout the 1950s, if they did work, nearly all women took traditional female jobs, becoming secretaries, waitresses, teachers, or nurses.

But would women settle for the way things used to be?

Portrait of Abigail Adams, late 1770s

Susan B. Anthony and Elizabeth Cady Stanton, 1899

The first women's rights convention was held at Wesleyan Chapel
in Seneca Falls, New York, July 19 and 20, 1848.

Our Roll of Honor

Containing all the
Signatures to the "Declaration of Sentiments"
Set Forth by the First

Woman's Rights Convention,

held at
Seneca Falls, New York
July 19-20, 1848

LADIES:

Lucretia Mott
Harriet Cady Eaton
Margaret Pryor
Elizabeth Cady Stanton
Eunice Newton Foote
Mary Ann M'Clintock
Margaret Schooley
Martha C. Wright
Jane C. Hunt
Amy Post
Catherine F. Stebbins
Mary Ann Frink
Lydia Mount
Delia Mathews
Catherine C. Paine
Elizabeth W. M'Clintock
Malvina Seymour
Phebe Mosher
Catherine Shaw
Deborah Scott
Sarah Hallowell
Mary M'Clintock
Mary Gilbert

Sophronia Taylor
Cynthia Davis
Hannah Plant
Lucy Jones
Sarah Whitney
Mary H. Hallowell
Elizabeth Conklin
Sally Pitcher
Mary Conklin
Susan Quinn
Mary S. Mirror
Phebe King
Julia Ann Drake
Charlotte Woodward
Martha Underhill
Dorothy Mathews
Eunice Barker
Sarah R. Woods
Lydia Gild
Sarah Hoffman
Elizabeth Leslie
Martha Ridley

Rachel D. Bonnel
Betsey Tewksbury
Rhoda Palmer
Margaret Jenkins
Cynthia Fuller
Mary Martin
P. A. Culvert
Susan R. Doty
Rebecca Race
Sarah A. Mosher
Mary E. Vail
Lucy Spalding
Lovina Latham
Sarah Smith
Eliza Martin
Maria E. Wilbur
Elizabeth D. Smith
Caroline Barker
Ann Porter
Experience Gibbs
Antoinette E. Segur
Hannah J. Latham
Sarah Sisson

GENTLEMEN:

Richard P. Hunt
Samuel D. Tillman
Justin Williams
Elisha Foote
Frederick Douglass
Henry W. Seymour
Henry Seymour
David Spalding
William G. Barker
Elias J. Doty
John Jones

William S. Dell
James Mott
William Burroughs
Robert Smallbridge
Jacob Mathews
Charles L. Hoskins
Thomas M'Clintock
Saron Phillips
Jacob P. Chamberlain
Jonathan Metcalf

Nathan J. Milliken
S. E. Woodworth
Edward F. Underhill
George W. Pryor
Joel Bunker
Isaac VanTassel
Thomas Dell
E. W. Capron
Stephen Shear
Henry Hatley
Azaliah Schooley

Souvenir card from 1908 listing the signers
of the Declaration of Sentiments in 1848

Photograph of Sojourner Truth

A women's suffrage information booth in New York City, 1914

Hundreds of women who support the suffrage
movement gather at the US Capitol, 1915

Alice Paul and other women celebrate the ratification
of the Nineteenth Amendment.

Alice Paul kneels by Susan B. Anthony's headstone, 1923.

Young women standing in the spinning room of a mill, early 1900s

Daisy Chain 1909

Students at Vassar College in Poughkeepsie, New York, 1909

Victoria Woodhull was the first woman to run for president.

War worker in a munitions factory, 1940s

A march celebrating the fiftieth anniversary of
women's suffrage in the United States, 1970

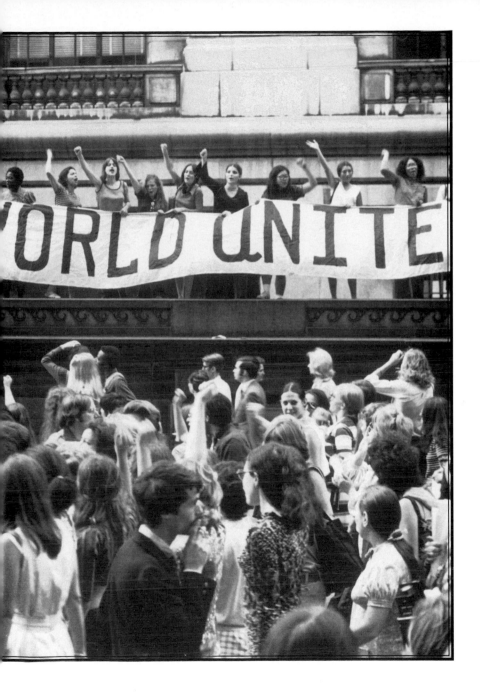

Shirley Chisholm announces she will run for president, 1972.

Gloria Steinem sits at her desk during a staff meeting for *Ms.* magazine, 1975.

Betty Friedan (left) at a conference promoting the Equal Rights Amendment, 1977

United States swimmers hold up their gold medals
at the Rio 2016 Olympic Games.

Hillary Clinton campaigns during the 2016 presidential election.

Protesters march on Pennsylvania Avenue during the
Women's March in Washington, DC, on January 21, 2017.

Women's March in Washington, DC, on January 21, 2017

Maya Angelou (1928–2014)

One black teenager was determined to get the job she wanted. Maya Angelou lived in San Francisco and wanted to be a streetcar conductor. At first, she was not allowed to apply, but she kept showing up day after day. In the end, she became the city's first black streetcar conductor. Later, she grew up to be an award-winning writer. In 1993, Maya Angelou read a poem at the inauguration of President Bill Clinton, becoming the first African American and first female poet to do so.

CHAPTER 10
The Second Wave

After World War II, there was an economic boom in the United States. Soldiers and sailors came home to attend college and take jobs. They married, bought homes, and started families, leading to a big generation of children called "the baby boomers."

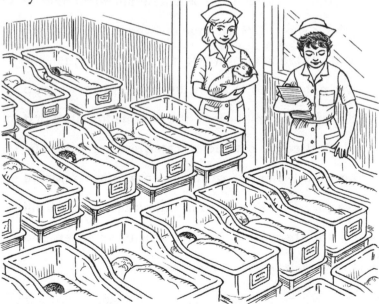

The ideal woman of the 1950s was no longer Rosie the Riveter but a homemaker devoted to her husband and children. New processed foods like sliced cheese and frozen meals saved her time in the kitchen. Women had dishwashers, vacuums, and other appliances to make cleaning easier.

In 1950, only about 29 percent of women worked outside the home. More single women worked than those who were married. As before, higher percentages of black women, whether single or married, were in the workforce. But all working women shared something: They were paid less than men.

The government-sponsored childcare of the war years had ended. Married women had an especially hard time combining work and family.

Betty Friedan

That was true for a woman named Betty Friedan. Betty had grown up in a Jewish family in Illinois. Born in 1921, she graduated from Smith College (another Seven Sisters school) in 1942. Then she got a job as a journalist. But when she became pregnant with her second child, she was fired.

Betty began writing from home, selling articles to magazines. After returning to Smith College for her fifteenth class reunion, she began asking her former classmates some questions about their lives. She found that many had comfortable lives but were unhappy. She said, "American women were frustrated in just the role of housewife."

Women wanted more freedom to choose their paths in life. They wanted families *and* careers. No one had been talking about this publicly. Betty called what women were feeling: "The Problem That Has No Name." In 1963, she turned her ideas into a best-selling book called *The Feminine Mystique.*

Betty received a flood of letters from readers. She said, "I realized that it was not enough just to write a book. There had to be social change."

So in 1966, she cofounded the National Organization for Women (NOW). It launched the "second wave" of the women's rights movement. Like the movement of the nineteenth century, it mostly was driven by white, middle-class, well-educated women. Many of them (and some men, too) began to think of themselves as *feminists*—people who believe in the equality of the sexes in all aspects of life—public and personal. They wanted to be able to plan their families, and have the chance to pursue careers to become lawyers, surgeons, professors, and scientists.

Black feminists also became active at this time. Many African American women felt that neither the women's rights movement nor the civil rights movement addressed important issues that mattered to the experiences of women of color.

Alice Walker

Some black feminists at this time included author Angela Davis, who wrote about women, race, and class. Novelist Alice Walker became a leader in exploring the impact of racism and culture on black women. In 1972, lawyer Florynce "Flo" Kennedy helped nominate New York Congresswoman Shirley Chisholm to run for president. Chisholm was the first black woman elected to Congress and also the first African American woman to run for president.

Shirley Chisholm

In the early 1970s, Gloria Steinem was called "the face of feminism" and a trailblazer of the second wave of the women's movement. She was born in 1934 in Ohio. Like Betty Friedan, she attended Smith College and worked as a journalist. As an editor of *New York* magazine, she published the first stand-alone issue of *Ms.* magazine in January 1972. Its feminist motto is "More than a Magazine, A Movement."

Gloria also helped start the National Women's Political Caucus, which works to increase women's participation in politics and provide support for women running for office. In 2017, at age eighty-three, Gloria was still giving speeches.

The second wave of feminism helped bring about many changes in society. Many barriers for women were broken. In 1981, Sandra Day O'Connor became the first woman to serve as a judge on the Supreme Court. (In 2017, three of

the nine judges were women.) Geraldine Ferraro was the first woman to run for vice president on a major party ticket in 1984. In 2007, Nancy Pelosi became the first female Speaker of the House of Representatives in Washington, DC. In 1997, Madeleine Albright became the first woman secretary of state. (By 2009, two other women—Condoleezza Rice and Hillary Clinton—had also held this job.)

In an interview in 1992, when she was seventy-one, Betty Friedan reflected, "The women's movement is an absolute part of society now." Betty died on February 4, 2006, her eighty-fifth birthday.

CHAPTER 11
Title IX Changes the Game

In 1972, a US law transformed the lives of millions of American girls and women. It is called Title IX.

Title IX is a federal law. That means it's the law in all states. It bans discrimination based on education. It is just thirty-seven words long. But Title IX guarantees that girls and young women can take part in all public school activities, many of which hadn't been open to them before.

It might be hard to imagine today, but before 1972, high school girls who wanted to take part in sports often could only be cheerleaders. Title IX changed that.

No longer could a school use all its money for sports on a boys' team. There had to be an equal share of money spent for girls' sports, too. The sports don't have to be the same for girls and boys. But there must be an equal opportunity to take part in them.

The results of Title IX have been dramatic. According to the National College Athletic Association (NCAA), in 1966, only about 15,000 women played team sports in college. By 2000, the total was 150,000 women—ten times more.

In 1971, girls made up only 7 percent of athletes in high school. By 2001, 41.5 percent of varsity athletes in US high schools were girls. During that time period, the number of girls in sports grew from about 295,000 to almost 2.8 million girls. What a change!

While most people think Title IX is only about sports, it actually does more. The law covers ten areas, including math, science, career education, education for pregnant and parenting students, and access to higher education.

Title IX means schools cannot forbid girls or boys from taking certain classes because of their sex. For instance, in the past, boys took classes related to tools and cars; girls took classes in sewing and cooking. A boy shouldn't face barriers if he wants to learn how to cook. A girl should be able to take classes to be a car mechanic, construction worker, or computer technician.

Many twenty-first century jobs are in STEM fields—science, technology, engineering, and math. There are still more men than women in these fields. To address this, Title IX asks schools to make sure STEM programs are open and welcoming to girls.

Title IX has already changed the lives of so many girls and women. The law has helped girls and women achieve their dreams—many have even gone to the Olympics. In 1900, at the

Olympic Games in Paris, France, only twenty-two of the 997 athletes were women. By 1960, over 20 percent of the participants at the Winter Olympic Games were women. At the 2014 Winter Olympic Games, women represented 40 percent of athletes. The numbers keep growing, too. In 2016, 45 percent of Olympic athletes were women.

The results of Title IX for American women are clear. At the 1972 Summer Olympics in Munich, the year the law passed, American women won twenty-three medals while US men won seventy-one. At the 2016 Summer Olympic Games in Rio de Janeiro, US women won sixty-one medals compared to fifty-five for men.

Thanks to Title IX and more support for girls in athletics, American girls and women are competing against the best in the world—and winning!

CHAPTER 12
Going Forward

Since 1776, when Abigail Adams picked up her pen to call for women's rights, American women have made tremendous gains. But there is much to be accomplished for women to achieve full equality with men.

On average, American women are still paid less than men. In 2016, the overall gender gap was 20 percent. That means female workers make only eighty cents for every dollar earned by men. Also, Native American, African American, and Latina women earn lower salaries than white and Asian American women. Feminists continue fighting for fair pay for *all* women.

Many women remain in jobs considered "women's work," which have lower pay and

Congresswoman Maxine Waters is an advocate
for women and people of color

fewer benefits. Women are also not promoted to leadership positions nearly as often as men. The term "glass ceiling" is used to describe an invisible barrier that keeps women and minorities from getting the top jobs at a company.

A White House report indicated that: "In 2014, only 4.8 percent of CEOs [chief executive officers] at Fortune 500 companies were female . . . This is due in part to the persistence of barriers for women in business that exist at each step of a woman's path to a business career, leading to the loss of women from business careers at each step."

What are these barriers? Some people point to the "old boys' network." This means men tend to mentor and promote other men.

Also, there are fewer women in advanced business programs, called *MBA programs*, than men. Female MBA graduates do begin their careers at the same pay level as men. But a 2015 White House report showed that after working for five years, "men earned approximately 30 percent more than women, and, after ten or more years, this gap stretched to 60 percent."

It's true that women have made gains serving in government at the local, state, and national levels. The first woman elected to Congress was Jeannette Rankin of Montana in 1916. A record 108 women served in the 114th Congress (2015–

Jeannette Rankin

2016), with eighty-eight in the House and twenty in the Senate.

According to a 2015 White House report, between 1916 and 2015, a total of 313 women were elected or appointed to Congress. Of these, 202 were Democrats and 111 Republicans. Thirty-eight African American women, eleven Hispanic women, and ten Asian Pacific American women have served in Congress.

While the number of women in Congress changes with each election, it lags below the percentage of women in our nation. That's why the Institute for Women's Policy Research has concluded that women won't hold an equal number of seats in Congress for another one hundred years!

The United States definitely lags behind other countries in this area. A 2017 report showed the United States ranked 101 out of 191 countries in female representation in national legislatures. Eleven nations, including Rwanda, Bolivia, Sweden, Mexico, South Africa, and Nicaragua, had more than 40 percent of women in their national legislatures.

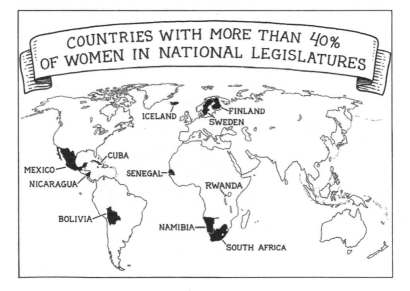

COUNTRIES WITH MORE THAN 40% OF WOMEN IN NATIONAL LEGISLATURES

In 1872, Victoria Woodhull became the first woman to run for president. Over the next fifty years, more than a dozen other women tried but failed to capture the nomination of a major political party. That is, until 2016.

After Barack Obama served two terms as the first African American president, many people were hopeful that in the 2016 election a woman could break "the highest glass ceiling"—and win the presidency of the United States.

Barack Obama

One woman was ready to try—for the second time. Former First Lady, US senator, and secretary of state Hillary Clinton came close. She accepted the Democratic Party nomination for president in July 2016.

Hillary Clinton (1947–)

Hillary Clinton was born on October 26, 1947, in Chicago, Illinois. She attended Wellesley College,  where she graduated as senior class president in 1969. Hillary received a law degree from Yale in 1973, and married her classmate Bill Clinton in 1975. (He was US president from 1993 to 2001.) They have one daughter, Chelsea.

After her years at the White House, Hillary became a senator from New York (2001–2009). She tried running for president in 2008 but lost the Democratic nomination to Barack Obama. President Obama appointed Clinton as secretary of state, the third woman to hold that position, serving from 2009 to 2013. In 2016, Hillary became the first woman to become the presidential nominee of a major political party.

In November 2016, Hillary Clinton won the popular vote by nearly 2.9 million votes, but fell short in the Electoral College. That meant she lost the election. The day after her loss, Hillary made a speech.

She said, "I know we have still not shattered that highest and hardest glass ceiling, but someday someone will, and hopefully sooner than we might think right now."

American women heard those words. And just as they had in 1913, women decided to march on Washington during inauguration week. On January 21, 2017, about a half million people gathered in the nation's capital. A total of five million people participated in Women's Marches in the United States and around the world.

In her speech the day after losing the election, Hillary Clinton had special words for all girls in America. Her words remind us what the women's movement is all about.

Hillary said, "You are valuable and powerful and deserving of every chance and opportunity in the world to pursue and achieve your own dreams."

Timeline of the Women's Rights Movement

1776 — Abigail Adams urges her husband to "remember the ladies"

1848 — First convention for women's rights held in Seneca Falls, New York

1872 — Susan B. Anthony is arrested for voting in a presidential election

1913 — Women march for suffrage in Washington, DC

1920 — Nineteenth Amendment, giving women the vote, is ratified

1932 — Amelia Earhart is the first woman to fly solo across the Atlantic

1955 — Rosa Parks is arrested for refusing to give up her seat on a segregated bus in Montgomery, Alabama

1963 — Betty Friedan publishes *The Feminine Mystique*

1966 — National Organization for Women (NOW) is established

1972 — Title IX bans gender discrimination in schools

1981 — Sandra Day O'Connor becomes first female Supreme Court Justice

1983 — Sally Ride becomes the first American woman in space

1987 — Congress establishes March as Women's History Month

2016 — Democrat Hillary Clinton is the first woman presidential nominee of a major party

2017 — Millions join the Women's March in Washington and across the nation and world

2018 — Second annual Women's March takes place on January 20th in cities across the United States

Timeline of the World

1776 — Declaration of Independence is approved

1788 — United States Constitution is ratified

1789 — George Washington inaugurated as first president

1861 — Civil War begins

1863 — Emancipation Proclamation frees slaves in Southern states

1869 — Fifteenth Amendment, extending voting rights to black men, is passed

1900 — Women take part in the Olympic Games for the first time

1903 — Marie Curie is the first woman to win a Nobel Prize

1911 — The Triangle factory disaster leads to workplace improvements

1917 — United States enters World War I

1941 — United States enters World War II after the attack on Pearl Harbor

1979 — Margaret Thatcher becomes the first woman prime minister of Great Britain

1993 — Toni Morrison is the first black woman to win the Nobel Prize in Literature

2005 — Angela Merkel becomes the first woman chancellor of Germany

2006 — Ellen Johnson Sirleaf becomes president of Liberia and first elected woman leader of an African nation

2015 — Elizabeth II becomes Britain's longest reigning monarch

Bibliography

*Books for young readers

*Bausum, Ann. *With Courage and Cloth: Winning the Fight for a Woman's Right to Vote*. Washington, DC: National Geographic, 2004.

Evans, Sara M. *Tidal Wave: How Women Changed America at Century's End*. New York: Free Press, 2003.

Flexner, Eleanor, and Ellen Fitzpatrick. *Century of Struggle: The Woman's Rights Movement in the United States*. Cambridge: Harvard University Press, 1996.

Ginzberg, Lori D. *Elizabeth Cady Stanton: An American Life*. New York: Hill and Wang, 2009.

*Hopkinson, Deborah. *Susan B. Anthony: Fighter for Women's Rights*. New York: Aladdin, 2005.

Kleinberg, S. J. *Women in the United States, 1830–1945*. New Brunswick: Rutgers University Press, 1999.

Laughlin, Kathleen A., and Jacqueline L. Castledine, editors. *Breaking the Wave: Women, Their Organizations, and Feminism, 1945–1985*. New York: Routledge, 2011.

MacLean, Nancy. *The American Women's Movement, 1945–2000: A Brief History with Documents*. Boston: Bedford/St. Martin's, 2009.

McMillen, Sally G. *Seneca Falls and the Origins of the Women's Rights Movement*. New York: Oxford University Press, 2008.

*Mountjoy, Shane. *The Women's Rights Movement: Moving Toward Equality*. New York: Chelsea House, 2008.

*Pollack, Pam, and Meg Belviso. *Who Was Susan B. Anthony?* New York: Penguin Workshop, 2014.

*Robbins, Dean, and Nancy Zhang. *Miss Paul and the President: The Creative Campaign for Women's Right to Vote*. New York: Knopf, 2016.

Stern, Madeleine B. *We the Women: Career Firsts of Nineteenth-Century America*. New York: Schulte Publishing Company, 1962.

Wertheimer, Barbara Mayer. *We Were There: The Story of Working Women in America*. New York: Pantheon, 1977.

Wheeler, Marjorie Spruill, editor. *One Woman, One Vote: Rediscovering the Woman Suffrage Movement*. Troutdale, OR: NewSage Press, 1995.

Yellin, Emily. *Our Mothers' War: American Women at Home and at the Front During World War II*. New York: Free Press, 2004.

Websites

www.haudenosauneeconfederacy.com

www.iwpr.org

www.jbhe.com/chronology/

www.now.org

www.nwhm.org/

www.smithsonianeducation.org/educators/resource_library/
women_resources.html

www.womenshistorymonth.gov

www.nps.gov/wori/